At the Art Museum

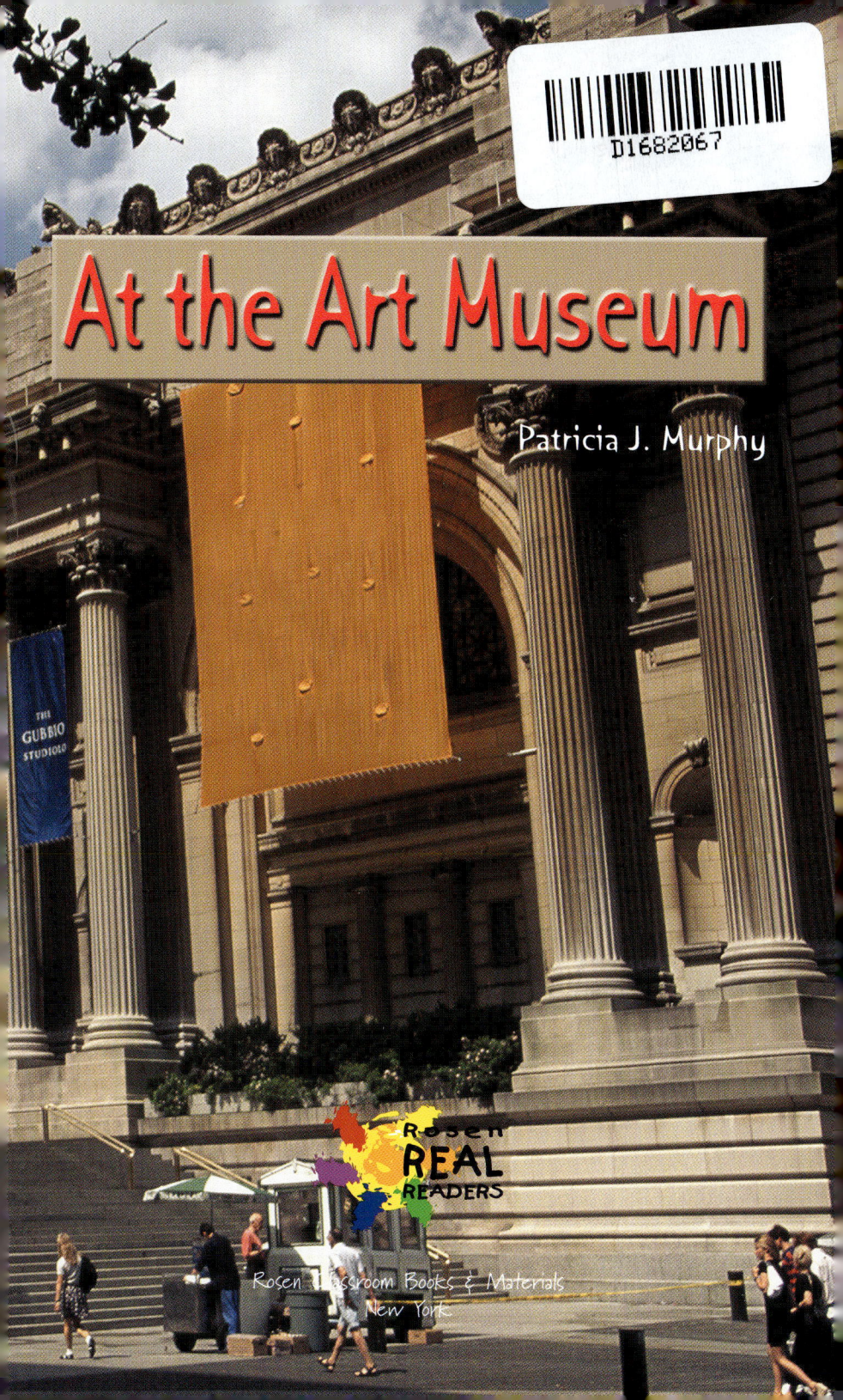

Patricia J. Murphy

Rosen Classroom Books & Materials
New York

Published in 2003 by The Rosen Publishing Group, Inc.
29 East 21st Street, New York, NY 10010

Copyright © 2003 by The Rosen Publishing Group, Inc.

All rights reserved. No part of this book may be reproduced in any form without permission in writing from the publisher, except by a reviewer.

Book Design: Haley Wilson

Photo Credits: Cover, p. 1 © Bob Krist/Corbis; pp. 4, 11, 12 (inset) © Stone; pp. 6–7 © Stan Ries/International Stock; pp. 12–13 © The Image Bank; p. 8 (Rodin) © Michelle & Tom Grimm/International Stock; p. 8 (Monet) © Archivo Iconografico, S.A./Corbis.

ISBN: 0-8239-6375-6
6-pack ISBN: 0-8239-9557-7

Manufactured in the United States of America

Contents

The Art Museum	5
Why We Visit Art Museums	6
Paintings, Sculpture, and More!	9
Where the Art Comes From	10
People at the Art Museum	13
How to Visit an Art Museum	14
Glossary	15
Index	16

4

The Art Museum

An art museum is a special building. Paintings and **photographs** hang on its walls. **Sculptures** fill its spaces. This art is made by different artists. The artists made the art in different ways. The museum will keep its art for many years.

Most art museums are open all year so you can look at art whenever you want to.

Why We Visit Art Museums

Art has always been an important part of people's lives. A long time ago, people drew pictures in caves before they could write words.

Art museums show art from different artists, countries, and times in history. This art gives people different views of the world. It may make them feel certain things. It may make them think or see things in new ways, too!

Some people like to study the people and objects shown in artwork. Others like to think about how the art makes them feel.

7

Monet
The Morning

Rodin
The Thinker

8

Paintings, Sculpture, and More!

Every art museum has different artwork. A museum might have paintings by Monet (moh-NAY), sculpture by Rodin (roh-DAN), and photographs by Ansel Adams. Each painting, sculpture, or photograph is a work of art. A museum's works of art are shown in **galleries**. Special **exhibits** (egg-ZIH-bits) sometimes show art for only a short time.

With so many works of art in a museum, people are sure to see something they like.

Where the Art Comes From

A museum's art comes from different places. Some works of art are gifts to the museum. Others are bought at art **auctions** (AWK-shuns). The art comes from all over the world.

Museum **curators** (CYUR-ay-ters) decide what art the museum will buy and show. They help their museum's art collection grow.

Curators are very busy people. They have to take care of many things at the art museum.

11

12

People at the Art Museum

Many people work in an art museum. All of the workers at the art museum work as a team. Some help show art or keep it safe. Others help visitors learn about art. Some plan **tours** or fix paintings. Some hang paintings on the walls or change lightbulbs.

◀ Art museums also have people who build and design galleries and exhibits.

How to Visit an Art Museum

Here are a few tips for visiting an art museum:

1. Get a museum map. Maps help visitors find their way around.

2. Take tours. Tours teach visitors about the art they see.

3. Just walk around and make your own discoveries!

Glossary

auction — A sale where things are sold to the people who offer the most money.

curator — A person at a museum who takes care of the art and decides what art to put in the galleries.

exhibit — Objects or pictures set out for people to see.

gallery — A place where art is shown to the public.

photograph — A picture taken with a camera.

sculpture — A form made out of clay, rock, wood, or metal.

tour — To visit and learn about a memorable or historic place.

Index

A
Adams, Ansel, 9
art auctions, 10

C
collection, 10
curators, 10

E
exhibits, 9

G
galleries, 9
gifts, 10

H
history, 6

M
Monet, 9

P
painting(s), 5, 9, 13
photograph(s), 5, 9
pictures in caves, 6

R
Rodin, 9

S
sculpture(s), 5, 9

T
tours, 13, 14

W
world, 6, 10